Bulw

and

Basfc

on old picture postcards

Grenville Jennings

1. The approach to Bulwell Market Place from the Nottingham direction. The open-top tram has just come down Highbury Road, having passed St. Mary's Church. No indication of who published the card, which was sent to Walsall in November 1908.

Designed and published by
Reflections of a Bygone Age,
Keyworth, Nottingham 1993
*Reprinted 1994, 1996, 1997, 1998 and
2001*

ISBN 0 946245 70 3

**Printed by
Adlard Print and Typesetting Services,
Ruddington, Notts.**

2. A multi-view card published by W.H. Smith. Each picture was also available as an individual postcard.

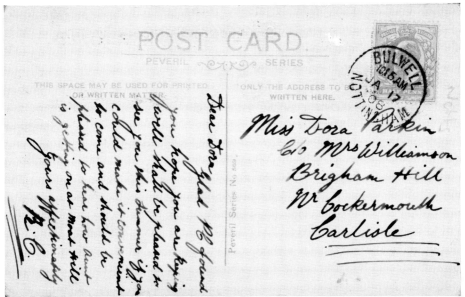

3. Picture postcards were the favoured way of communication with friends and relatives in the Edwardian period: cheaper than a letter, and easily available, with a huge variety of pictures to send and collect. It was to be many years before the telephone was accessible and affordable to the mass of ordinary folk. The picture side of the card has a view of Main Street with *'Greetings from Bulwell'* in embossed lettering.

INTRODUCTION

The purpose of this book is to portray Bulwell and Basford through the medium of picture postcards, which were at the height of their popularity in Edwardian times - both as items on which to send messages and as pictures to collect.

Picture Postcards were first published in Britain in 1894, but it was not until a decade later that they began to take off, when in 1902 the Post Office allowed a message to be written on the address side. This meant that the whole of the one side was available for the picture, which obviously gave more scope to the publishers.

Photographic viewcards became very popular and the postcard became the most important way of communicating news or messages in much the same way as the telephone is used today. The years up to 1914 were the 'Golden Age' of picture postcards, when millions of cards portraying every imaginable subject were published by a host of national and local firms. Hardly a village or hamlet was not documented at that time by a postcard publisher, though sometimes the number of cards available was unrelated to the size of a community.

The majority of cards illustrated in this book were produced by local firms which is really only to be expected. The publishing giants of the age published fine cards of towns and city centres and tourist locations, but with a few exceptions - notably W.H. Smith - were reluctant to venture into the suburbs and villages.

One of the most prolific publishers of early local cards was Albert Hindley, who ran a stationery shop on Clumber Street in Nottingham (currently occupied by Granada TV Rentals). He issued the "Clumber" series of postcards covering much of Nottingham and the surrounding area. These date from around 1905 and were printed in colour by a firm in Glasgow. Another local publisher well-represented on the following pages is C. & A.G. Lewis.

What is striking about many of the cards is the relatively empty streets. Some photographers obviously rounded up local children to provide some animation, but the majority of the cards highlight the atmosphere of the early part of the century, when traffic outside the bigger towns was very limited.

Postally used cards with messages on can prove both interesting and informative, and the views themselves provide endless fascination. A house gone here, a railway bridge no longer there, tree-lined roads unrecognisable with the disappearance of the trees. How we take things for granted.

As the present slips into the past almost un-noticed, picture postcards are a fine reminder of how things used to be. It is hoped that the following pages will allow both young and old to wallow in a little nostalgia of early Bulwell and Basford.

Grenville Jennings
March 1993

Acknowledgements: to Tim Farr for the loan of cards 14, 29, 35 and 36, and to Peter Cooke for the loan of cards 1 and 19.

Front cover (top): marvellous group of Edwardian children at the Bull-Well on a 'Peveril' series card no. 566, sent from Bulwell to Ashbourne in January 1908. *"This is a PC for your collection",* wrote the sender.

Back cover (top): montage postcard of St. Mary's Church and schools, posted in 1912.

(bottom): Photographic view of Lincoln Street crossing, Basford, on a C. & A.G. Lewis-published postcard.

4. This 'Rex' series card (no.727) was sent to Louth in August 1928. *"I am having a jolly old time"*, wrote Mr. Wain. Boots the Chemists' shop is on the extreme right of this picture, with the Maypole Dairy Co., Hickman (family butcher), and C.B. Edwards, also in evidence. A tram on route no.3 (Trent Bridge - Bulwell) waits to set off, while in the road, a policeman appears to be directing non-existent traffic. Almost all the men in view are wearing a hat.

5. Looking further down Main Street, with Boots now in the centre. W.H. Smith card, posted from Bulwell in August 1915.

MARKET PLACE, BULWELL, NOTTINGHAM

6. W.H. Smith postcard (no.210) taken from Main Street. Pedestrians wander happily around the Market Place with no vehicles in sight apart from a stationery tram. Hilton's store is now on the left.

TRAM TERMINUS, BULWELL. NOTTS.

7. The tram terminus, Bulwell with car no.11 ready to depart for Trent Bridge. Prosser & Co's clothiers shop is to the left on Market Side. Another W.H. Smith postcard, posted to Aylesbury in August 1910.

8. Tram car no.1 on the number 3 service rests in Bulwell Market Place with J. Hickman's shop in the background. A privately-published card of 1920s vintage. This service, which had begun in July 1901, finally closed in May 1934.

9. Main Street, Bulwell. The building marked with a cross is the former Methodist Chapel, which in its day was such an important building that dignitaries like the mayor, and sheriff of Nottingham, laid foundation stones in August 1882. Another W.H. Smith card, sent to the Isle of Man in August 1912, and featuring a street so deserted that ladies can stroll down the middle of the road!

GREETINGS FROM BULWELL.

MAIN STREET, BULWELL, NOTTINGHAM.

10. A view of Main Street (with figures superimposed on an empty scene!) serves as a greetings card from the town. 'Peveril' series card, postally used in January 1908.

Main Street, Bulwell, Nottingham.   Peveril Series. 3070

11. 'Peveril' series card of Main Street, 1912, with traffic confined to bicycle, horses and carts.

12. Fifty years later, and a postcard view by A.W. Bourne of Leicester. A van delivering Be-Ro flour is parked near the zebra crossing outside the co-operative stores. Traffic is still minimal.

13. The new Salvation Army building in Bulwell dates from 1908. On this anony-mously-published card, posted to Skegness in 1909, Lottie writes *"you would not care to come here for a day, would you? A day excursion is 2s 9d G.N.R."*

14. The Reading Room in the Public Library, situated next to the Police Station on Quarry Road. The local bobby is on guard on this postcard sent from Bulwell in June 1910. A bigger library was built later on Highbury Vale. *(see illus. 33).*

QUARRY ROAD, BULWELL, NOTTS

15. Quarry Road (re-named Commercial Road in 1913) on W.H. Smith card no.108. On the left, at the corner of Pilkington Street, is Eastmans Ltd, the national butchery chain.

QUARRY ROAD, BULWELL, NOTTINGHAM.

16. Another view of Quarry Road, this time on a 'Peveril' series card of c.1910, with the Public Reading Room on the right.

17. The River Leen at Bulwell on 'Peveril' series card no. 520, posted from Nottingham in December 1906.

THE RIVER LEEN, BULWELL NOTTINGHAM.

18. The river bank is crowded with children all smartly dressed on this W.H. Smith postcard.

19. Cinderhill Road, Bulwell, on an anonymously-published photographic card. The railway line to Cinderhill Colliery passes over the road here.

20. Bulwell's cemetery gates and offices were laid out by the Public Parks and Burial committee in 1903. The cost, including improvements to Hempshill Lane, the approach road, was £10,130. 'Peveril' series card no.367, posted in July 1908.

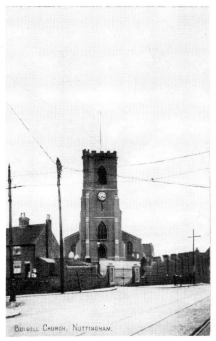

BULWELL CHURCH, NOTTINGHAM.

21. St. Mary's Church was designed by H.J. Stevens of Derby and built in 1850. 'Clumber' series card no.156.

22. The site of the Bull-Well was on Bestwood Road. The name possibly originated from an early word for the bubbling of the water of the well, or possibly the Anglo-Saxon name 'Bulla'. Whatever the reason, it was a hugely popular spot with children, as evidenced on this W.H. Smith postcard. The Midland railway line runs behind the fences.

109   BULL WELL, BULWELL, NOTTS.

The Well, Bulwell.   Blakey Bros., Ltd., Printers, Nottm

23. Another view of the Well on a postcard published about 1903 by Blakey Bros. Ltd., of Nottingham.

110   SQUIRE'S LANE LEADING TO BULWELL. HALL. NOTTS.

24. Squire's Lane is shown on W.H. Smith card no.110, posted at Bulwell in June 1913. *"Arrived very late after a tiring journey"*, wrote Ethel, *"have been exploring and found Auntie and she took me to see Rock Cemetery."*

-15-

THE LODGE, BULWELL HALL, NOTTS

25. The Lodge at the entrance gates to Bulwell Hall on a 'Clumber' card, published about 1908 but not actually used until April 1930. At 574 acres, Bulwell Hall Park was the largest of Nottingham's public parks.

103   BULWELL HALL, BULWELL NOTTS.

26. Bulwell Hall was built in 1770 by John Newton as a residence for the Lord of the Manor. In 1908 the Hall and Park was bought by Albert Ball and sold to Nottingham Corporation for £35,000. The land has since been used as a public park and golf course. The Hall was demolished in 1958. W.H. Smith published this card, mailed to Staffordshire in July 1915. *"The park is simply glorious, with grounds for all sorts of games"*.

27. The beautiful flower garden at the Hall is featured on 'Clumber' series card no.57.

28. Bulwell Salvation Army Band on a card published in the early 1920s by C. and A.G. Lewis.

29. Postcard by Nottingham firm C. &
Market Place is dominated by Boots th

ace, Bulwell. No. 255

ewis published in the early 1920s. The
hists and Hiltons Boot and Shoe Shop.

30. The Ladies' Pavilion at Bulwell Golf Links on 'Clumber' series card no.29, posted from Nottingham in June 1906. *"I have not sent one like this before: you must tell me if I have..."* wrote Ada.

31. Notts Golf Club set up links on Bulwell Forest in 1887, when the course had just seven holes. These were extended in 1894 to a full eighteen-hole circuit. This W.H. Smith postcard, sent from Bulwell in 1913, shows golfers in action.

32. An astonishingly high turn-out of residents were photographed for a card published by Widdowson during floods in 1910. Flooding was a regular occurence, due to the River Leen overflowing!

33. C. & A.G. Lewis postcard sent to Skegness in August 1924 shows off the public library on Highbury Vale to good effect.

34. The photographer on Highbury Vale has attracted a crowd of onlookers eager to feature on the postcard. 'Peveril' series no. 3069, posted from Bulwell in August 1915.

35. Highbury Vale on a card published by Spree, postally used at Bulwell in June 1926. This view is taken from the corner of Ingram Road, and the shop on the immediate right is that of confectioner John Warren at no.174. Further up, at no. 180, is Wm. Horry's tailors shop.

36. A view of Highbury Road on an anonymously-published card of about 1908.

37. Methodist Sunday School procession of Edwardian vintage.

38. Postcard of a school festival in Bulwell Market Place, August 1911, sent by George to his mother at Ashton-Under-Lyne later that year. *"That was our minister who is speaking in the trilby hat..."* He's not the only one with an impressive hat – a fine array of them is evident on this picture.

39. Another Sunday School procession, here seen on Highbury Road, with St. Mary's Church in the background.

40. Sunday School parades gave everyone a chance to dress up in their best clothes, and photographers took group pictures in the knowledge they had a captive market for the postcards.

41. Photographic postcard by a Mr. Flavell of 248 Highbury Road, showing a factory interior somewhere in Bulwell about 1910. The card was probably produced in small quantity, and is relatively rare. A possible location might be the Bulwell Finishing Co.

42. Empire Day (c.1912) is celebrated at the National Schools, Bulwell. The schools were built in 1865-6 to accommodate 518 children on the site of the village green at a cost of £3,000.

43. The National Schools were located on Main Street, just beyond Ragdale Road. Another Empire Day photograph, with class 1 boys saluting the flag. Alfred Bainbridge is at the front.

WILLIAM RIGLEY'S RAILWAY WAGON WORKS BULWELL

44. Interior view of William Rigley's Railway Wagon Works at Bulwell. The card was posted to F.R. Howe & Co., Newport in 1906, advising them that a repair to one of their wagons was completed.

45. Bulwell Cricket Club in 1908 on a card published by O.J. Reardon of Bulwell.

46. Midland Railway Station, Bulwell, on a 'Peveril' series card mailed to 190 Highbury Vale in December 1906. Otherwise known as Bulwell Market, it was on the line between Nottingham and Mansfield, fifteen minutes from the former and forty minutes from the latter. In 1910 there were typically thirteen stopping trains in each direction, with two extra on Saturdays. The last evening train left Nottingham Midland at 11.15 and, running non-stop, reached Bulwell in eleven minutes. Bulwell Market station closed to passengers in October 1964.

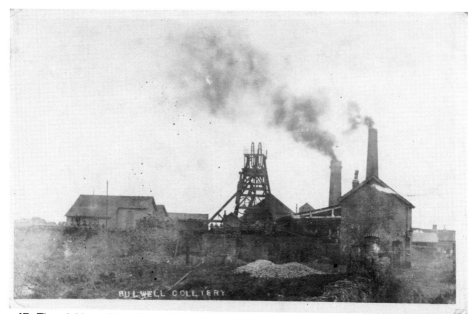

47. The sinking of the Cinderhill and Bulwell pits in the 1840s turned Bulwell into a coal mining area, and by 1914 as many as 66% of the working inhabitants were believed to be involved in the industry. Photographic card of Bulwell Colliery, posted to Boston in January 1908.

48. 'Clumber' series card of the railway crossing at Lincoln Street, Basford, showing an open-top tram passing the bottom of Southwark Street on the Bulwell-Trent Bridge route. The card was sent to an address in Radford in October 1912.

VERNON ROAD. BASFORD. NOTTINGHAM.

49. A sunny Vernon Road, Basford, on a 'Peveril' postcard sent to Tring in Hertford-shire in August 1931.

BASFORD WAKES 19

50. Basford Wakes was located on waste ground between Vernon Road and Lincoln Street, known locally as "Billy Bacons". This lively scene comes from the 1906 fair.

51. Two shoe repairers working for James Coombes & Co. pose outside the shop on the corner of David Lane and Lincoln Street. One of the notices read: *"Hand sewn repairs – gents 3/6d, ladies 2/6d per pair"*. This photographic card dates from about 1908.

52. A cobbled Lincoln Street, Basford, with the "up-to-date fish & chip saloon" on the right, and the "Butchers Arms" on the left.

Parish Church, Nottingham (Basford).

53. The Parish Church of St. Leodegarius, Basford, in the 'Peveril' series no.515, posted to Talbot Street in Nottingham in June 1908. *"Hope you have not got this view,"* wrote the sender.

54. The pawnbroker was an essential part of life in the early twentieth century. This card shows the premises of E. Toft on Church Street, Basford, about 1910. Men's jackets are advertised at 1/3d each.

55. Basford House on a 'Peveril' series card. Amongst the owners of the house, which was built about 1730, was Thomas Bailey, proprietor of the *Nottingham Mercury* and his son Philip, a celebrated poet whose epic *"Festus"* was written in the house in 1839. Postcard sent to Hove in May 1908.

56. The 'White Swan' Inn, Basford, on the corner of Church Street and Alpine Street.

ARCHWAY, L N E R STATION, BASFORD AND BULWELL, NOTTINGHAM

57. Basford and Bulwell station was originally on the Great Northern line connecting Derby and Nottingham via Kimberley and Ilkeston. In 1923 it was amalgamated into the London and North Eastern Railway Company. This card in the 'Peveril Real Photo' series shows a mixed train crossing the archway over Vernon Road about 1927. Highbury Road is on the other side of the archway, while the Northern Baths are on the left just before the bridge. Posters on the roadside advertise, among other products, Maltanop and Chivers' jam. The station was closed to passengers in September 1964.

G. STANLEY & SONS,

ESTIMATES FREE.   ESTABLISHED 1883.

REMOVALS TO ALL PARTS OF THE COUNTRY
:: BY EXPERIENCED PACKERS. ::

58. Postcards were also used as an advertising medium, as illustrated on this card promoting G. Stanley & Sons of New Basford.

59. Stone-laying ceremony at the start of the building of Basford's Parish Church Hall on May 25th, 1905. Postcard sent from Old Basford in July 1905.